Animal Offspring

Penguins and Their Chicks

Revised Edition

by Margaret Hall

CAPSTONE PRESS
a capstone imprint

Table of Contents

Penguins 4

Eggs 8

Penguin Chicks 12

Growing Up 18

Watch Penguins Grow 20

Glossary 22

Read More 23

Internet Sites 23

Critical Thinking Questions 24

Index 24

Penguins

Penguins are birds that
use their wings to swim.
They cannot fly.
Young penguins are
called chicks.

Penguins come to land
to mate and lay eggs.

Eggs

Female penguins lay one to three eggs. Some penguins keep their eggs on their feet. Other penguins keep their eggs in a nest.

Most penguin parents take turns keeping the eggs warm.

Penguin Chicks

A penguin chick hatches from the egg. Chicks have soft feathers called down.

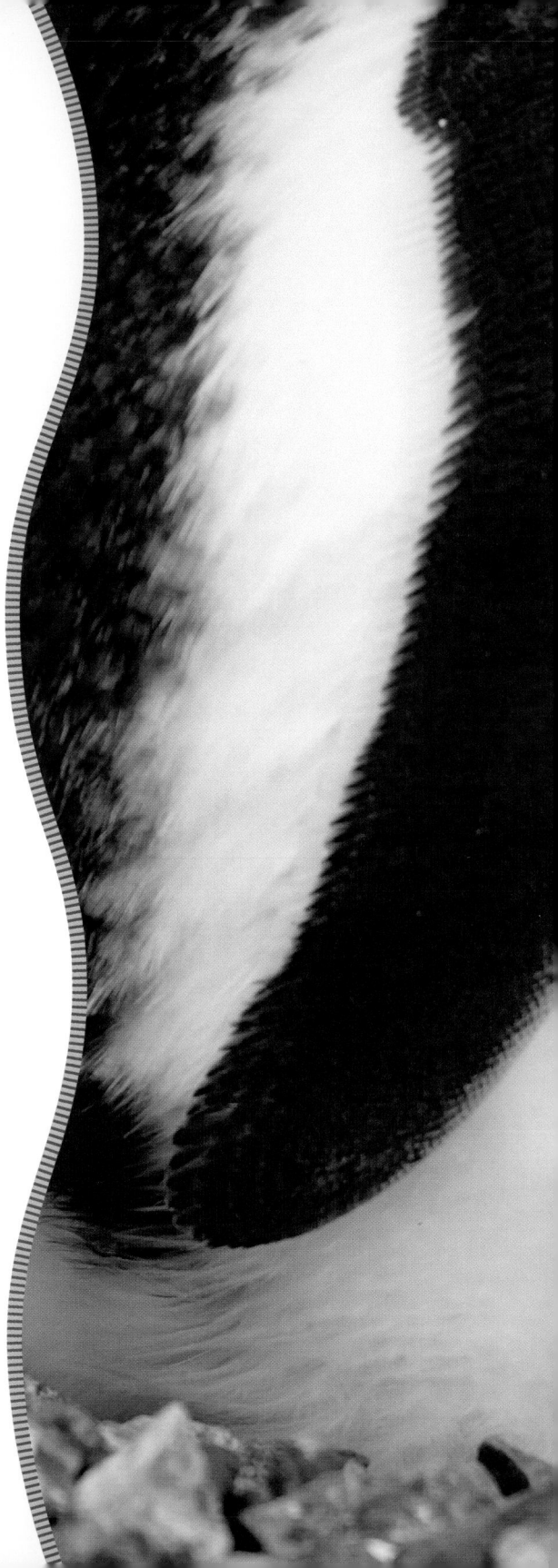

Penguin parents catch fish
for the chicks to eat.

Sometimes the chicks stand together to keep warm. Chicks grow new feathers after a few months.

Growing Up

Most penguins can swim and take care of themselves after about one year.

Watch Penguins Grow

hatching

adult after
about five years

Glossary

bird—a warm-blooded animal with wings, two legs, and feathers; birds lay eggs; most birds can fly

down—the soft feathers of a baby bird; young penguins with down cannot swim until they grow new feathers; the new feathers are waterproof

hatch—to break out of an egg; a young penguin has an egg tooth on its beak; it uses the tooth to help it break the egg open

mate—to join together to produce young; some penguins come back to the same place every year to mate

nest—a place built to raise young; some penguins make nests; other penguins keep their young warm on their feet or by using their feathers

wing—one of the feather-covered limbs of a bird; most birds move their wings to fly

Read More

Beer, Julie. *Penguins vs. Puffins.* Washington, D.C.: National Geographic Kids, 2017.

Salomon, David. *Penguins.* Step into Reading. New York: Random House Books for Young Readers, 2017.

Schuh, Mari. *Penguins.* Black and White Animals. North Mankato, Minn.: Capstone Press, 2017.

Internet Sites

Use FactHound to find Internet sites related to this book.

Visit *www.facthound.com*

Just type **9781543508253** and go.

Critical Thinking Questions

1. What does a penguin use its wings for?
2. Where can you look to find information about down feathers in this book?
3. How does standing together keep penguins warm?

Index

birds, 4
chicks, 4, 12, 14, 16
down, 12
eating, 14
eggs, 6, 8, 10, 12
feathers, 12, 16
feet, 8
females, 8
fish, 14
flying, 4
hatching, 12
land, 6
mating, 6
nest, 8
parents, 10, 14
swimming, 4, 18
wings, 4